An Epic Epicurean Feast, book 2,
To celebrate the life of Ashley ‘Jack’ Scarborough

As the ghost of Ash disappears
I remember more, as he asked me
not to fear
But write a feast of knowledge
He inspired me to learn
As to find the solution to poverty
In the world
As a bet for his soul
His redemption and resurrection

Japanese rice is sushi, expensive
Yet Thai rice is cheap
A wonder at how to raise agriculture
And poor farmers can have more
than karma
As what is valued and what profit is,
From Ricardo to Marx
Executed in food architecture
Architexture of three types of taste
Or feeling of food into our lives

Yet in Africa's poor, can all the babies
    and children have more toys?
Division in mathematics does not exist
    more than a ring or a field
In the farms did Che Guevara fight
And brought one light of socialist gloom
Each person in the field
    is given micro-Barclay card
We should be building assets
    for the poor rather than loans
As country after country falls
    from debt, then premise-singer
thesis, as out flows the lifeblood of the
economy, a functionalist duality,
Economists think they have the answer

As unfettered and free market
Yet why is there not enough food in the
market?
Policy is stories, narratives of 1 level
Not a pagoda or a tower
It's all just about maintaining power
And so some are made lower
And the fisherman is not a rower

As Adam Smith thought this would
mean more production,
And everyone is from him, induction
The crucial example is Argentina
Which was rich once, then came to a
crisis, and low again.
North Korea was first capitalist state
Before South Korea's agricultural rural
mural of production relations,
Then we see Marx's prediction of
natural development, in a world where
someone can't be pregnant
For a free thought is a baby
And grows to full maturity,
Keep apart each policy pair
And come to a dialectic to stop despair,
That vested interest and billowing
financial winds
Bring people to argue against the social,
Because who would clean the bins?
Pay the bin men more, the trash
Need not feel everyone rash
Ash was the answer
And life was the question

As I found the life that suits me
“Suits you sir” Ashley said
But what to do with Edward Said,
A prey or kind?
Myth from Levi-Strauss
Is the core of our modern world
As the myth is an ordering of the world around us,
There is no loss of generality
Instead of wars and generals
Bombs and scares
Forever afraid of Lion’s lair
Defence as a shot in the arm for economy
When people suffer and fear
The government should do more than protect its own rear,
Looking into a rear mirror to drive
The economy mad like a child in the back looting and fighting its brother!
Everything is lies, that I write and surmise,
Because the Library is full of all the books, and is a Lie-Lie.

How do you spell Phd?
What does knowledge mean to me
Bourdeoui talked of symbolic and
cultural capital, to plug you into the
system of babylon, a phone, a car and
internet connection.
Yet the direction of society is the
Liberty to pursue profit
When bosses are unfit
The world becomes

What is the vision of the governments,
From data does it see
A spectacle from the sea
Of possible thought
It's all wrong, all the numbers
As even a growth in population
Is not really known
Statistics is brought in
And makes more capitalist clones
The world moans
Yet it has given loans
And makes everyone poor
The cold street of bones

Much less a growth in GDP
The money, the profit, the
productivity,
As this is all value-added
While being told to be in values
Can value of sharing come together
For the government's preparing
Weary homeless are wearing
Don't shed a tear
Don't tear the two alpha's for a gamma
on the same page of work,
As to Cambridge universe we lurk
The politics should be people's dreams,
Yet with leaven is the luxury of falling
And if you give me the luxury of failing,
I finish my work, yet to labour all does
come together, a ground of value,
Then a pont de capiton of captives,
In your house, beyond the road's bars,
Only to go out to the bar,
And having it large.

Wether the weather is good
Or bad

Comes from nonlinear dynamics
And
Lorenz attractor.

The arrows of the weather report
Make a grouping, I would have thought,
As the air is ever looping
And the seaman in the sea, is rower
Ships meeting at knight
A bird flying in skies bright
All these show a constraint
On atmosphere's, many spheres
Not Daint,
Can the rises and throuffs in
relationship,
Be ever an attractor to flight
As I leave the dream of ashley
And come to my daze about a girl-she,
As in language we reproduce another,
Who is a change in the word's meaning,
Not meaning to be mean!
A birth of sea, a river to flow beneath
me,
Haydn the creation

You know the score
As in a Genesis of law
Of physics and pythons
Did humble Satan in her lifetime
Is our love a paradise lost
As we are left away in feelings-raw

A rise and fall of the orchestra
Crescendo then silence
As music takes us to the door
What is the key?

Scaling a scale, like fish
Like a guitar strumming
Gives the world what is bliss
And often missed

Melody, higher, To Rhythm then
lower, To Chord Progression,

Melody, higher, To Rhythm then
lower, To Chord Progression,

Melody, higher, To Rhythm then
lower, To Chord Progression,

Scales - as a subset; chords and keys
Then Harmony.

The harmonious society.
A secret sect of music, musically.

Then together in a HExagon.
But what is the invariant set?
As a leviathan eating up Jonah
Wailers and moaning rock music
Male female play of signs and pont
de capiton
A lake of Lacan and Blake
Run now from the drake.
If music could hold all
And not just be a wedding song
Leading women to marriage
And music plays in music hall

Music as more than an intuition
As we marry the beat in our heart

To the melody of a repetition
Rep is important for the star
Yet the cold moon plays on the lyre

I feel Ashley is alive in me
I feel alive in Ash
It wasn't all about the cash
That's one interpretation
Yet dreams abound in the world
And nightmare is our only station

Black and white, wearing the same suit,
Marker pen on the clothes
Lips of red and rose
Arise a nation suffered so many blows,
Put your hands in your pocket
As beautiful are your eyes in socket
The background is a colourful affair
As image and soul are women fair
The picture of a shoe
Like a prince coming through
To fit a slipper on a already worn foot
The arches of a church,

as two people come together as a face,
A bed of grass and a handbag
The Druid in Stonehenge with flags
Golden dress
A poignant face, look full of grace
As the lace underwear
Brings lions to the lair
Liar, Liar, Liar

Stockbrokers in a broke economy
Wandering herds of goats
Drinking from castle's moat
Sire, Sire, Sire

Pretty Little Upstarts
Plough Big Startups
how do we push the idea up a level
In streets and fields we revel
Bouncing to tunes
While i play in a fountain
And in my dress am wet
The aesthetic of zones
The life worlds all blown

Knots in a string
That makes everything
The basics of science
Is this really a reality?
Can I escape from samsara
Can I find nirvana?
Can I go to Heaven
with all this leaven
As my heavy bags need one thing
To be left alone then I sing
Who needs to look good?
We need culture more than couture
Fencing as a fight, into a prison
Yet Ashley is risen
No more do I feel alone
No more regrets and moans
Just the thought of a koan
What is your original face?
The one you had before you were born?
This koan is the first step on a long
and hopeful journey
Where you need to be strong
Many can write Ash's words

But only flight comes to all the birds
Desire, a short film
Delight, a slow embrace
Death, the finality,
    or the beginning of a great adventure.
Watch it now on
www.brightonpavilion.co.uk
Break the caste and the cask
Go about to find forgiveness,
    just ask.
Forget about your own ass
And think of all others
As to be bethroded is your goal
No more feminism in jail.

Love, Love, Love

The face of a woman
All covering the page
With just eyes and mouth
Lips I kiss
By looking at it

The word love is over the face
And my eyes on hers
I trace,
Richness is a merit
Yet comes from banks in hedges
As the garden of the money world
Is in mathematics all a swirl
The lashes of the eye
Driving away from babylon
But still rooted in the perception
A sentiment of scrutiny as a
philosophy,
Functionalism, for a function
The nose is blurred
On the picture ash made for me
A line in an upside down crucifix
Lips red and pink, enclosing teeth
Beautiful white teeth
The tooth hurts,
But what is truth?
Truth is pretty, falsehoods petty
A hula-hoop spiralling round my
waste,

A saint in a topless photo shoot
Nipples against chain mail
Loved by men, the species male
Yet she has a job
Wearing a bandana round her forehead,
Hand is hidden away in pocket
Eye's a looking intense,
                I brought it,
Sitting on a designer black chair
Resting is luxury
And luxury leads to the fall of
civilisation,
All is noise beneath the chair
A fuzzy picture on a television of old
Where does the hand of law touch?
Or rather torture, too much
Law is rent, a value of values,
        thought to be heaven sent,
I scent the world wants more
As if to our dreams we do adore
We all want a job,
Yet honour is also important
Were I a man to rob

Honour leaves me, then i am a
hierophant,
Altogether is Ash's alone
I'm scared to be skin and bones
A sin in a rash
Never thought to anyone
A hashishin, from old times in Egypt
In Crusades and knights and more
As the world came later to the pursuit,
of more
To avoid such clashes
To abore all the lashes
Yet the face of a woman
Can yet bring love and tension
In a world of a story of a journey
Through the goal of Hades,
When in this travel was unravelled
A string in a maze,
A string theory to amaze
Music spacing skills of steps
Drum and bass music;
Beats 1, 3, 5, 9, 11, 13
With snares and aires of grace
On my wax I do trace

Yet below this is the rhythmic bars
Of copied and sampled music
To make another song
That is just played along
By a skillzi dj
Remonstrating on the mix
A little forward
The same tune played for ever
The same sound louder than ever
Of cries for the earth and nature
It seems natural now, such a river
That joins the seas, John ‘o the pleased,
Robin Hood was a noble man
The same thing happens when people rebel,
I would rather look at Hayden
From intellect we all are hiding
Creation as Genesis
The Lord rested made the weekend party,
As you see the archetype of such malarkey,
The echo in history,
An alternative to the counter-factual

Yet putting time to time
- dt/dt
you get something sublime
As time causes itself yet is only a moment,
- dt = f(t) is what you end up with
In time man is in loss
Except the past and the future
With knowledge of this
Bringing a safety from the Fates,
Yet phat beats make you have
Rhythm
A secret to service everyone
As to our ends we could be done
By government and not retirement
Tired I feel writing these words
That flow from me
The minute I ponder on Ashley.
Do you want sugar with that
No thanks, I'm sweet enough!
Do you want salt o'er the Earth?
I am too bitter.
A chain rule of dt/dt?
I wonder positively?

I wander, the wand and the worn
W- whatever!
A- Andrew neal
N- Nothing
D- Daleth please
W and what? Can we make mathematical sense of?
All you know is he was there,
Nothing to nothing
Your evil loses you your soul
The evil thoughts of judging
The crime of punishment
The lemons you eat all day
The cold, not the warm
As to beaches everyone does swarm
And leaves the Psalms, the song
The leafy woods I travelled through
With ash and climbed trees like some fools,
We called to people at the bar opposite,
And broke too much to go there too (2),
We talked of women and worrying
We wandered the tree to see our bretherin, no time for bread to rise

As to the time of ancient Egypt I did appear in,
Ands talked to Pharoah, showing the answer to his evil
Tests, Test, TESTS!
Bob Marley's Exodus melded into the bible's chapter Exodus
A movement of ja-people,
Jah as Jehovah
Rattle and run over
By science that seeks to predict
Yet not guide
That's why spirituality of all kinds
Can we abide,
I'm sparkling, I'm a Parker Ray,
PArker Lewis can't lose,
Each new idea, new seed
Becoming a sapling of maturity
When it is ready to fit into other ideas
And theory is fitting, Fit it into others,
A marriage of messages,
To be a carriage to the sages
Of old and new
If it is a good idea, then leave it

Look only at inferences from it,
Do not spend a theory's political capital in excess,
Gorging on truth, When the stomach is falsehood,
And wasting each seed's potential
To make a forest
Not a jungle
Whilst not a stately home's garden
And fields.
And encourage support to confer on the thinker's their idea.
Do not entrust knowledge to those weak in understanding,
As weakness is not just lack of strength,
But of the mind, beyond soul and heart,
Knowledge is timeless
Clothe the poor, and maintain an external shell, to the thoughtless.
Textiles for tax on the tiles
Ta- ta- tata, ta
Test, lies, a theory of fashion,
From Fascism,
Memetic theory, meme's seen

As the fashionista is now a barista,
As we wake up,
A buck for a coffee?
A taste of freedom in a key
Innately,
Not the key to a home
Just to wander on the streets, all alone
Yet what if everyone was a troubadour?
Bolder and bolder would we be
As society seeks strength, will and riches,
From lands away from each other
Yet from visiting them, you find yourself,
Do we really need all this wealth
When we're happy with less
Instead a caress, L.O.V.E
The haters can make like Bees
As an Eris, a Loki, a mischief of chiefs,
Too many chefs spoil them both,
Thesis and antithesis among many theories, lines of debate and circles of knowledge.
Split them up into families of theories

And do not mate with an idea it's
previous incarnations,
Rather than a traffic jam of bifurcations,
Between lost ideas and knowledge
Interfering yet not fearing
Cheers Big Ears,
Lend me your noddy,
Robed in and robbed of all reason
As a drunk walking down the road in
season,
Blackened the way, so near to fun
As every day's gift is your choice
Without it, just rejoice
And what is Justice?
Criminals in courts, caught red handed,
All law is subjudice on subjudice
And everyone is also that
For law guides everyone
And its revolution is a circle

The same from mirror neurons
Which give healing and learning
An aesthetic at least
Of equality, and like the balance

Gives broken hearts an arrest

Justice as the balance
Music equal to music
A melody in Bach

A compensation to beats and sounds
A progression to a higher form
Fear not the law
With ash there is nothing to fear

As the demons pass around you
And you extinguish your ego
They fade away and become as
everything is in samsara,
emptiness and void
Like a bounced cheque
Like chess with the greats
The two knights together next to
two pawns,
Is king and queen, should you still feel
solorn,
A journey to plenty,
That the goal the tree villages in the sky,

Where people live and rejoice in a tribe,
Of environmentalism and scribe,
You are who you ascribe to be,

Entropy and it's balancing out
    in an ecology
Ericlitese the philosopher said
    no one steps in the river twice
Yet between shaila and charibus is the
single vector of Plato's ship
The captain driving the trajectory
Does a ship travel twice in its movement
As goods and chattels go to and fro
Between China to England
Then back again
There and back again;
    A Hobbit's adventure
And the ring of trajectory
Makes a whole new story
As I waken from where i was layn
And go to church for praying
Yet the door is shut
For those who dissent
Disorganised religion

All along a vector of morality
Avoid the trap of the ring
Just in your heart sing
Words of old? Words of new?
The old was better
As people were not fatter
A diet, St Francis of Assisi
Non-coveting, existing in nothing
Esse calls can give hope
The Enochain watchtowers
As a prayer
The Sigil Del Ameth
A crucifix to bear
Bless yourself and all others
Then says some words of old
A Flibble rather than a Fible
And tell your little fib's
To Ash as he judges your weight of sin
and carbon neutrality,
Planting a tree that grows to
everywhere,
Leaving your past life behind
And saying where you did lie

Heraclitus said no one steps in the
    same river twice,
Yet no one steps in the river once,
Endless threads and weaves of flow
Water as plaited hair
Where it was is gone, giving way to
more than this and that,
Still time's arrow exists,
But is wrong, 30 years is it from a
father's son to become a maker of
children,
30 names the days of a moon
From new to middle to old moon
The geometric progression of life
    and population
When the phases of moon are
subjective,
The relation between scientific evidence
and theory, moon to population,
Kant would have said, analytical and
synthetic knowledge
But what can build bridges?

The cosmos works by harmony and
tension, the lyre's many strings versus
the bow's single string,
So Fourier is wrong!
Air dies giving birth to fire,
Water is born of tired earth,
Yet water meets fire in destruction.
Of both.
So too the world, all is flux
And we hold onto what love there is,
too much.
Yet too little love and too much, are they
a Derridian contradiction of opposites,
As the philosopher on his haunch does
sit,
And the hyper reality fires missiles
missed, surely we can think of fish
As David to Goliath,
Philistines! Barbarians! The other of
itself,
From the High Elf
As people build islands on sea subsided
shelfs,

And give bread, and take it, to birds and pigeons, a little charity
To take from yourself clarity,
Fake the pieces of glass into your heart,
And make it as your art.

Flights of wonder as the crow flies,
A find of money, have steak ribeye,
Don't be a money bags,
Don't drag yourself into your millstone,
Rather find 30, milestones,
Two o'clock we go for a walk,
Binah and chockma
As you reach a barrier
Simply sit and celebrate ashley,
All the book of lies of Crowley
Are separated from this epic
Or you could just do a picture
And show and tell the world of your rapture,
A rupture in the soul between our purpose and our environment,
Order needs myth, and truth is rhetoric,
Without the sun, what day! What night!

As one is for true and another for false,
Yet are the same sun.
So too are interdependent equations
A Jacobian of lean and fat years
Endless cycles that are one sun
And who has won?
And who has fun?
As fun is what life's about.
And in Ashley there was no doubt
As this modern life brings no clarity
As you just end up on charity
Till Charon takes you across the sticks,
And demons on your mind play tricks
Fire penetrates my cigarette
And the proof of the trajectory of smoke
my mind does take,
As this is interdependent equations
An etra for a raison,
A true d'etat,
A rebellion that is an extinction
So dinosaurs rule again
You can take any time between any time
in statistics and data,
Making obfusticated and fatter,

Is the it the former or the latter,
I have always confusion about time,
The solution is the crown, yet this is a
nose to smoke,
Not a joke,
But something to fire's tales of folk
And camp fire, can we be tryers
        or truer?
The crown is the place where all things
derive, but what is crown in fire-water-
earth-air-fire?
Each one can be this pont de capiton,
And the words from this a-re legion
Two made one are never one, Heraclitus
said to me,
My grandfather's answer;
        1+1=11
Singing together we compete
And in this union there are several
types,
Of addition, multiplication and AND,
A paradox of infinite dimensions,
A dialectic from a dialectic
Yet not close to Aristotle's one

Time's arrow from dead wood, springing
back to life to end each one,
And a fountain of knowledge springs
from my muse,
Not to see truth as a refuse,
We must therefore recycle,
There in philosophy since time
immemorial,
And make nice gifts of 3 or more,
From old things made renewed and
glory,
Glory of the earth,
Holly is the Earth.

www.ingramcontent.com/pod-product-compliance
Ingram Content Group UK Ltd.
Pitfield, Milton Keynes, MK11 3LW, UK
UKHW020227250726
13967UKWH00001B/228